MW00682106

powerful
Encounters
with the real
Jesus

S U D D E N
I M P A C T

Reality Check Series

REALITY CHECK — SIX DISCUSSIONS

powerful
Encounters
with the real
Jesus

SUDDEN IMPACT

MARK ASHTON

WILLOW CREEK RESOURCES

ZONDERVAN™

GRAND RAPIDS, MICHIGAN 49530 USA

ZONDERVAN™

Sudden Impact
Copyright © 2002 by Willow Creek Association

Requests for information should be addressed to:

Zondervan, *Grand Rapids, Michigan 49530*

ISBN: 0-310-24522-2

Interior design by Sherri L. Hoffman

Printed in the United States of America

02 03 04 05 06 07 08 /❖ CH/ 10 9 8 7 6 5 4 3 2

To Caysie,
my precious little girl.
May Jesus' sudden impact
cause you to do "Craze-y" things.

CONTENTS

DOING CRAZY THINGS

Have you ever done something really crazy? Something you couldn't explain, but just felt compelled to do?

People did crazy things when they met Jesus. Whenever he crossed paths with people, he always had a sudden impact. Tax collectors gave money to the poor. Prostitutes changed careers and became faithful to only him. Children sat on his lap and danced and sang. Paraplegics walked home to see their families. Blind men saw beautiful sunsets. Dead people left their coffins and returned to life as normal. People sat for hours hanging on his every word. Roman centurions asked him for favors. One person spent a year's wages to buy perfume to spill on his feet. Some religious leaders worshiped him as God. Others became his murderers. After his death, his followers refused to deny him—even though it meant they would be tortured and killed.

What made people so devoted to Jesus? His teaching was unsurpassed among his contemporaries and stands as the model of excellence to this day. He healed the sick, cared for the poor, loved the loveless. He gave people hope, and provided tools for forgiveness and reconciliation in relationships. He understood the maladies of the human heart with crystal clarity and claimed to have the cure. He predicted the rise of a kingdom based on God's love and justice. He claimed to be God walking around in a human body.

But could all those things be true? Were these people merely hoodwinked by a fancy talking, charismatic leader? Fooled by a teacher who seemed to know the longings of the human heart and capitalized on them? Or merely touched by the kindness of a great man who seemed to care about everyone—children and adults alike?

You are about to embark on an adventure to decide for yourself. In this discussion guide, you'll encounter this same Jesus who made people do crazy things. You'll also meet six people—people whose lives changed suddenly and dramatically after meeting Jesus. A religion professor who was enlightened by the new teaching of the young master. *Impact.* Some roof smashers who destroyed a house to get a friend to Jesus. *Impact.* A dead man who walked out of the tomb at the mere sound of Jesus' voice. *Impact.* People on both sides of the law who recognized that he was the standard of goodness. *Impact.* A prostitute who became the model of religious devotion. *Impact.* Fishermen and tax collectors who left their businesses to wander around with this homeless healer. *Impact, impact, impact.* As each of these came face-to-face with the greatest life of all time, they couldn't help but be changed!

Within these pages are the very things that marked Jesus as who he was—and is. The things that made him seem so unique to the people of his day and even to us today. You'll find his message, some of his methods, and the results of his powerful greatness as it spilled into the lives of others.

In this guide, every high-impact encounter begins with an Icebreaker—a question or two that will stimulate your thoughts and make it easy for you to share your ideas and opinions, even with people you may not know very well or at all. You'll read words from the Bible that reveal each person's story, and then have the opportunity to discuss that story and life-change with others. Each topic ends with a Reality Check—a few questions that will help you apply what you've learned to your own life. And to understand the big picture of Jesus' life, you won't want to miss "Putting the Puzzle Together."

As you journey through this discussion guide, you'll see how Jesus' influence changed the lives of six people with vastly different backgrounds. You'll have the opportunity to walk in their shoes and see Jesus in the raw—like they did when he first clashed with his culture. You'll experience the tension between Jesus and religious leaders. And you'll stand close enough to the cross to hear the cries of loved ones and feel the uneasy pain of an unjust death.

As you observe Jesus interacting in all kinds of situations, you'll also find answers and hope for change in your own life. You'll learn the spiritual secrets Jesus revealed on a dark night on the side of a mountain. You'll discover how you can experience the healing power of Jesus. You'll find the keys to experiencing life beyond the grave.

And, hopefully, you too will laugh with Jesus, learn from him, and stand in awe of his power. Most of all, you'll discover why he's considered to be the most compelling figure in the history of the world! Perhaps after encountering him for yourself, you'll do some crazy things too!

THE PROFESSOR

ICEBREAKER

Watch a clip from the last scene of *Father of the Bride, Part 2.* In this scene, George Banks (Steve Martin) is in the hospital. Both his wife and his daughter, Annie, are in labor.

If you've birthed children, tell your best labor and delivery story. If you've adopted a child, tell about the "birth pangs" of paperwork, seeing first photos, and meeting that child for the first time. If you are not a parent, discuss where your parents (or friends) told you babies came from.

Read John 3:1 – 21

Now there was a man of the Pharisees named Nicodemus, a member of the Jewish ruling council. He came to Jesus at night and said, / ⊘1

"Rabbi, we know you are a teacher who has come from God. For no one could perform the miraculous signs you are doing if God were not with him."

In reply Jesus declared, "I tell you the truth, no one can see the kingdom of God unless he is born again." / → something unusual about his response? Q2.

"How can a man be born when he is old?" Nicodemus asked. "Surely he cannot enter a second time into his mother's womb to be born!"

Jesus answered, "I tell you the truth, no one can enter the kingdom of God unless he is born of water and the Spirit. Flesh gives birth to flesh, but the Spirit gives birth to spirit. You should not be surprised at my saying, 'You must be born again.' The wind blows wherever it pleases. You hear its sound, but you cannot tell where it comes from or where it is going. So it is with everyone born of the Spirit." / Q 3, 4

"How can this be?" Nicodemus asked.

"You are Israel's teacher," said Jesus, "and do you not understand these things? I tell you the truth, we speak of what we know, and we testify to what we have seen, but still you people do not accept our testimony. I have spoken to you of earthly things and you do not believe; how then will you believe if I speak of heavenly things? No one has ever gone into heaven except the one who came from heaven — the Son of Man. Just as Moses lifted up the snake in the desert, so the Son of Man must be lifted up, that everyone who believes in him may have eternal life. / Q 4 5

"For God so loved the world that he gave his one and only Son, that whoever believes in him shall not perish but have eternal life. For God did not send his Son into the world to condemn the world, but to save the world through him. Whoever believes in him is not condemned, but whoever does not believe stands condemned already because he has not believed in the name of God's one and only Son. This is the verdict: Light has come into the world, but men loved darkness instead of light because their deeds were evil. Everyone who does evil hates the light, and will not come into the light for fear that his deeds will be exposed. But whoever lives by the truth comes into the light, so that it may be seen plainly that what he has done has been done through God." / Q 8

DISCUSS!

1. What facts can we gather about Nicodemus from the first couple of sentences?

2. Jesus' initial response doesn't seem to go with the flow of the conversation. Why do you think he responded as he did?

3. Jesus and Nicodemus had very different views of the concept "born again." People today often mean something different from both of these options when they use the term "born again." Let's compare the ideas of Nicodemus, Jesus, and people today related to what being "born again" means. Fill out this chart together as a group.

What Does the Phrase "Born Again" Mean to You?

→ when they hear christians say "I'm born again"

Nicodemus	Jesus	People Today

4. What parallels are there between a "spiritual" birth and a "physical" birth?

5. Jesus is very strong and straightforward in his approach with this professor. If you were Nicodemus, how would you be feeling at this point?

DISCUSSION 1

6. "For God so loved the world that he gave his one and only Son, that whoever believes in him shall not perish but have eternal life. For God did not send his Son into the world to condemn the world, but to save the world through him" are some of the most famous words in all the Bible. Pick out all the action words (verbs) from these two sentences. When it comes to eternal life, what is God's role and what response does he desire from us?

7. Assume for a moment that Jesus' claim is true: that he is God's only Son. Would it then be arrogant for him to make the narrow claim, "Whoever does not believe stands condemned already"? Support your answer.

8. In this passage, light represents truth while darkness represents lies. A person moves into the light simply by living according to the truth. We all know someone who has been afraid of moving toward truth in at least one area of life. Tell of a time when you or someone you know (who should remain nameless) had a relational, emotional, or spiritual breakthrough by facing the truth.

REALITY CHECK

How would you compare your own search for God with Nicodemus' search? Explain.

___ Less academic
___ More straightforward
___ More relational
___ Less secretive
___ Less dogmatic
___ Other

more academic
less straight forward

80
12
16

12
8
960

500

doctor

Where are you in your understanding of spiritual life—still in the dark, moving closer to the light, or . . . (you fill it in)?

non-Xian
- carl
- Lyn
- Sherry
- tanya
- Lu.

THE ROOF SMASHERS

ICEBREAKER

Gather together a small stack of *Time, Newsweek, U.S. News and World Report,* or other news magazines. Page through the magazines and look for evidence in ads, articles, or pictures that we live in a messed-up world.

Read Mark 2:1 – 12

A few days later, when Jesus again entered Capernaum, the people heard that he had come home. So many gathered that there was no room left, not even outside the door, and he preached the word to them. Some men came, bringing to him a paralytic, carried by four of them. Since they could not get him to Jesus because of the crowd, they made an opening in the roof above Jesus and, after digging through it, lowered the mat the paralyzed man was lying on. When Jesus saw their faith, he said to the paralytic, "Son, your sins are forgiven."

Now some teachers of the law were sitting there, thinking to themselves, "Why does this fellow talk like that? He's blaspheming! Who can forgive sins but God alone?"

Immediately Jesus knew in his spirit that this was what they were thinking in their hearts, and he said to them, "Why are you thinking these things? Which is easier: to say to the paralytic, 'Your sins are forgiven,' or to say, 'Get up, take your mat and walk'? But that you may know that the Son of Man has authority on earth to forgive sins. . . ."

He said to the paralytic, "I tell you, get up, take your mat and go home." He got up, took his mat and walked out in full view of them all. This amazed everyone and they praised God, saying, "We have never seen anything like this!"

DISCUSS!

1. By this point Jesus is already getting a reputation as a great teacher and healer. How do the people of Capernaum respond to him when he arrives?

2. Imagine you are a person in the house where Jesus was teaching. Describe the sights, sounds, smells, and emotion.

3. What extreme lengths were the paralytic's friends willing to go to in order to get him to Jesus? What does this tell you about their attitude toward Jesus?

4. Judging by Jesus' reaction to the paralytic being let down, what did he see as the paralytic's greatest need, and why?

Today we often overestimate our own righteousness because we compare ourselves to other humans. But if we were to compare ourselves to God's moral perfection, we might grade ourselves a little lower. In order to understand something about God's standards, take a look at this "sin list":[1]

Lack of Love

Is there anyone against whom you hold a grudge?

Is there any person against whom you are harboring bitterness, resentment, or jealousy?

Do you quarrel, argue, or engage in heated discussion?

Are there people whom you deliberately slight or discount?

Do you have a complaining spirit?

Are you irritable, cranky, or impatient?

Have you recently been harsh or unkind?

Do you carry hidden anger?

Do you speak unkindly concerning people when they are not present?

Pride

Do you have a critical attitude toward any person, thing, or group?

Are your statements mostly about "I"?

Have you made a pretense of being something you are not?

Do you have a stubborn or unteachable spirit?

Do you insist on having your own way?

Are you more concerned about what people will think than what will be pleasing to God?

Impurity

Do you have any personal habits that are not pure?

Do you indulge in any pornography?

Do you allow impure thoughts about sex to stay in your mind?

Are you addicted to anything—food, television, pleasure, alcohol, drugs, sports, the Internet, etc.?

---

[1]Adapted from a message by Nancy Beach, New Community, Willow Creek Community Church, 2000.

Are you in any way careless with your body?

Is there anything (or anyone) you are jealous of?

Have you recently lied, exaggerated, or embellished the truth?

Do you follow through on your promises?

Spiritual Apathy and Laziness

Who is at the center of your life—you or God?

Is there anything in which you have failed to put God first?

Do you waste time or procrastinate?

Do you do your work "with all your heart"?

Do you have a thankful heart toward God?

Are you unwilling to obey God fully?

Is your life marked by too much busyness that keeps you from hearing or responding to God?

Are you honoring God with your finances?

Have you recently extended yourself in any way toward the poor, the imprisoned, the sick, or the elderly?

Are you getting enough rest, and practicing a day of rest and worship?

Do you have a heart of love for those you know who are far from God?

Are you filled with anxiety and worry?

Have you been a joyful person lately?

5. Compare your character to God's high standards. How do you measure up in each of the areas?

- Lack of love

- Pride

- Impurity

- Spiritual apathy and laziness

6. Jesus forgave the paralytic before he healed him, perhaps because he thought this was man's greatest need. Do you think forgiveness is everyone's greatest need? Why or why not?

7. Why were the teachers of the law irritated by what Jesus said?

8. Jesus asks a rhetorical question: "Which is easier to say . . ." Of the two options, it's obvious which one would be easier to see whether it came true or not. So why do you think Jesus poses this question at this point?

9. In what ways was Jesus convincing—or not—in demonstrating his authority to forgive sins?

REALITY CHECK

Have you—or anyone you know or have known—lived up to
God's morals for your whole life? For the past year? For the past
week? If not, how close are you?

All of us have sinned in some way or another. (That's why we
get that guilty feeling when we read over the "sin list.") But there's
good news: Jesus did not come to beat us up over our sins. As a
matter of fact, Jesus saw the forgiving of people's sin—yours and
mine—as his greatest mission on earth.

During the next week, remember the list of God's standards.
Keep track of how your life compares to them. And then imagine
how refreshing it would be to have them all wiped out of God's
record book through Jesus' forgiving power.

THE CORPSE

ICEBREAKER

Briefly describe a time in your life where you experienced significant pain (physical, emotional, or relational).

During that time, did God seem near, far, or somewhere in between—and why?

Read John 11:1 – 45

> Now a man named Lazarus was sick. He was from Bethany, the village of Mary and her sister Martha. This Mary, whose brother Lazarus now lay sick, was the same one who poured perfume on the Lord and wiped his feet with her hair. So the sisters sent word to Jesus, "Lord, the one you love is sick."
> When he heard this, Jesus said, "This sickness will not end in death. No, it is for God's glory so that God's Son may be glorified through it." Jesus loved Martha and her sister and Lazarus. Yet when he heard that Lazarus was sick, he stayed where he was two more days.
> Then he said to his disciples, "Let us go back to Judea."

"But Rabbi," they said, "a short while ago the Jews tried to stone you, and yet you are going back there?"

Jesus answered, "Are there not twelve hours of daylight? A man who walks by day will not stumble, for he sees by this world's light. It is when he walks by night that he stumbles, for he has no light."

After he had said this, he went on to tell them, "Our friend Lazarus has fallen asleep; but I am going there to wake him up."

His disciples replied, "Lord, if he sleeps, he will get better." Jesus had been speaking of his death, but his disciples thought he meant natural sleep.

So then he told them plainly, "Lazarus is dead, and for your sake I am glad I was not there, so that you may believe. But let us go to him."

Then Thomas (called Didymus) said to the rest of the disciples, "Let us also go, that we may die with him."

On his arrival, Jesus found that Lazarus had already been in the tomb for four days. Bethany was less than two miles from Jerusalem, and many Jews had come to Martha and Mary to comfort them in the loss of their brother. When Martha heard that Jesus was coming, she went out to meet him, but Mary stayed at home.

"Lord," Martha said to Jesus, "if you had been here, my brother would not have died. But I know that even now God will give you whatever you ask."

Jesus said to her, "Your brother will rise again."

Martha answered, "I know he will rise again in the resurrection at the last day."

Jesus said to her, "I am the resurrection and the life. He who believes in me will live, even though he dies; and whoever lives and believes in me will never die. Do you believe this?"

"Yes, Lord," she told him, "I believe that you are the Christ, the Son of God, who was to come into the world."

And after she had said this, she went back and called her sister Mary aside. "The Teacher is here," she said, "and is asking for you." When Mary heard this, she got up quickly and went to him. Now Jesus had not yet entered the village, but was still at the place where Martha had met him. When the Jews who had been with Mary in the house, comforting her, noticed how quickly she got up and went out, they followed her, supposing she was going to the tomb to mourn there.

When Mary reached the place where Jesus was and saw him, she fell at his feet and said, "Lord, if you had been here, my brother would not have died."

When Jesus saw her weeping, and the Jews who had come along with her also weeping, he was deeply moved in spirit and troubled. "Where have you laid him?" he asked.

"Come and see, Lord," they replied.

Jesus wept.

Then the Jews said, "See how he loved him!"

But some of them said, "Could not he who opened the eyes of the blind man have kept this man from dying?"

Jesus, once more deeply moved, came to the tomb. It was a cave with a stone laid across the entrance. "Take away the stone," he said.

"But, Lord," said Martha, the sister of the dead man, "by this time there is a bad odor, for he has been there four days."

Then Jesus said, "Did I not tell you that if you believed, you would see the glory of God?"

So they took away the stone. Then Jesus looked up and said, "Father, I thank you that you have heard me. I knew that you always hear me, but I said this for the benefit of the people standing here, that they may believe that you sent me."

When he had said this, Jesus called in a loud voice, "Lazarus, come out!" The dead man came out, his hands and feet wrapped with strips of linen, and a cloth around his face.

Jesus said to them, "Take off the grave clothes and let him go."

Therefore many of the Jews who had come to visit Mary, and had seen what Jesus did, put their faith in him.

DISCUSS!

1. What information can you gather from this story about Jesus' relationship with Mary, Martha, and Lazarus?

2. Compare the disciples' reactions to going back to Judea with Jesus' response. Why is Jesus not as concerned?

3. Martha believed that if Jesus would have come immediately, he could have stopped Lazarus from dying. If you were Martha, how would you respond to Jesus when he finally showed up—with Lazarus dead and cold in his grave?

4. After Jesus tells Martha her brother will "rise," he makes a startling claim. What is the double meaning of this claim?

5. Jesus didn't cry when he first got news of Lazarus' death—two days earlier. But he cries when he sees Mary and her friends. Why do you think that is?

6. Describe the situation as Jesus prays—the sights, sounds, smells, mood of the people. How might the mood change as Lazarus came out of the tomb?

7. Jesus made a startling claim and promise: "I am the resurrection and the life. He who believes in me will live, even though he dies; and whoever lives and believes in me will never die." And he dramatically supported his words by demonstrating his power over death. He asked Martha point-blank: "Do you believe this?"

How about you? Check the statement that best reflects your belief on this matter:

I think:

___ Jesus and Lazarus were magicians who played a hoax on people.

___ Something supernatural happened, but Jesus was not in control.

___ This story was probably made up centuries later by overzealous followers of Jesus and attributed as history.

___ The entire group must have been hallucinating that Jesus raised this guy from the dead.

___ Jesus did something amazing here, but it doesn't prove anything about his divinity.

___ Jesus clearly demonstrated his power over life and death.

___ He must be God's Son!

___ Other

8. How does this action of raising a person from the dead validate Jesus' claims to be the "resurrection and the life"?

REALITY CHECK

How does the fact that God weeps when his friends are in pain affect the way you view God in the midst of the crises you mentioned in the Icebreaker time or life's current crises?

Compare your spiritual life to the story of Lazarus. Where are you right now?

❑ Still in the grave
❑ Watching the stone being rolled away
❑ Alive but still in the grave clothes
❑ Alive and unwrapped
❑ Partying with the family and the crowd

Why?

SOLDIERS AND CRIMINALS

ICEBREAKER

Much can be learned about a person not only by the way they live but the manner in which they die. Some people die with love and dignity, while others spiral into bitterness and resentment.

Tell about a person you knew who was in his or her last days. What did you learn about that person by the way he or she handled mortality? Or briefly describe a memorable movie scene related to people facing death.

Before you read this next story about Jesus and how he interacted with soldiers and criminals, here's some helpful information you'll want to know: Saying that Jesus has had a rough week is a major understatement. He came to Jerusalem with hundreds of thousands of others during the week of the Passover (the biggest celebration in the Jewish year). After being hailed as a coming king and going through public verbal tussles with the religious leaders, he was unjustly accused of being a criminal. After enduring a farce of a trial and getting sentenced to death, he was publicly beaten and scourged.

Now Jesus is in the midst of the most difficult day of his life. He knows he's about to die—and in the worst way possible. Crucifixion is the most cruel and painful death ever devised as a means of capital punishment. The person's hands and feet are nailed to a cross, and it's torture for that person to try to keep himself upright in order to breathe. After a while the body grows too weak to hold itself up, and the person slowly suffocates to death.

When you read the following words, keep in mind that Jesus is enduring this kind of excruciating pain. How does he handle the distress and agony of his final moments? Let's take a look.

Read Luke 23:32 – 49

Two other men, both criminals, were also led out with him to be executed. When they came to the place called the Skull, there they crucified him, along with the criminals — one on his right, the other on his left. Jesus said, "Father, forgive them, for they do not know what they are doing." And they divided up his clothes by casting lots.

The people stood watching, and the rulers even sneered at him. They said, "He saved others; let him save himself if he is the Christ of God, the Chosen One."

The soldiers also came up and mocked him. They offered him wine vinegar and said, "If you are the king of the Jews, save yourself."

There was a written notice above him, which read: THIS IS THE KING OF THE JEWS.

One of the criminals who hung there hurled insults at him: "Aren't you the Christ? Save yourself and us!"

But the other criminal rebuked him. "Don't you fear God," he said, "since you are under the same sentence? We are punished justly, for we are getting what our deeds deserve. But this man has done nothing wrong."

Then he said, "Jesus, remember me when you come into your kingdom."

Jesus answered him, "I tell you the truth, today you will be with me in paradise."

It was now about the sixth hour, and darkness came over the whole land until the ninth hour, for the sun stopped shining. And the curtain of the temple was torn in two. Jesus called out with a loud voice, "Father, into your hands I commit my spirit." When he had said this, he breathed his last.

The centurion, seeing what had happened, praised God and said, "Surely this was a righteous man." When all the people who had gathered to witness this sight saw what took place, they beat their breasts and went away. But all those who knew him, including the women who had followed him from Galilee, stood at a distance, watching these things.

DISCUSS!

1. If you were enduring the pain of crucifixion, how would you treat the guards who were drilling nails into your wrists and ankles?

2. What is Jesus' response to the guards' actions, and what does this reveal about the purpose for his life and death?

3. Name the people who are at the crucifixion. How does each treat Jesus?

4. Contrast the two criminals on the cross. What assumptions about Jesus does each make?

5. Reflect on Jesus' response to the second criminal. What did the criminal do to deserve Jesus' favor?

6. How good and moral do you have to be to come to God?

7. What can people who hesitate to approach God because of their own sense of guilt learn from the criminal?

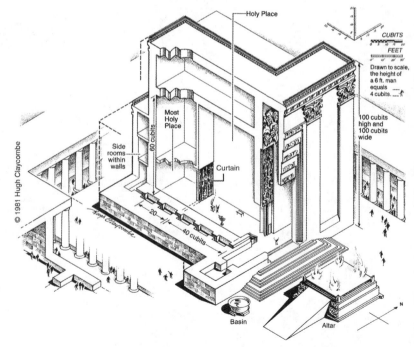

Holy Place

CUBITS

FEET

Drawn to scale, the height of a 6 ft. man equals 4 cubits.

Most Holy Place

100 cubits high and 100 cubits wide

Side rooms within walls

60 cubits

Curtain

© 1981 Hugh Claycombe

20

40 cubits

N

Basin

Altar

When Jesus dies, the curtain of the temple is torn in two. What does this mean?

Here's some background information: In the center of the temple in Jerusalem was a room called "the Holy of Holies." It was thought to be the place where the very presence of God dwelt. The high priest was the only one who could enter—and even he could only go in once a year. The room was separated from the rest of the temple by a floor-to-ceiling cloth curtain that was six inches thick. No one dared to go past the curtain for fear they would be consumed by the presence of God. The curtain was symbolic of the dramatic separation of common people from a Holy God.

8. What does the tearing of the curtain symbolize—and what does it mean for how we can relate to God?

9. Most likely the centurion had overseen dozens, maybe even hundreds, of crucifixions. Why would Jesus' behavior be so stunning to him?

REALITY CHECK

Two thousand years ago, scores of people gazed at Jesus on the cross with very different reactions: some scorned him, while others had pity. Some challenged his claims, while others began to believe them. Many just didn't care. Yet some turned toward Jesus, and a few even placed their faith in him.

What is your personal reaction as you envision Jesus hanging, bruised and bloody, breathing his last on a Roman cross?

Imagine it's true that we now have direct everyday access to God, rather than having to wait for the intermediary of a priest—and that only once a year. What differences does this make in your day-to-day world?

THE PROSTITUTE

ICEBREAKER

What things do you find it easiest to blow money on? Dinners out? Shows? Cars? Big toys?

To whom do you like to give extravagant gifts? Relate a story or two of when you gave an extravagant gift (or someone gave one to you).

Read Luke 7:36 – 50

Now one of the Pharisees invited Jesus to have dinner with him, so he went to the Pharisee's house and reclined at the table.

When a woman who had lived a sinful life in that town learned that Jesus was eating at the Pharisee's house, she brought an alabaster jar of perfume, and as she stood behind him at his feet weeping, she began to wet his feet with her tears. Then she wiped them with her hair, kissed them and poured perfume on them.

When the Pharisee who had invited him saw this, he said to himself, "If this man were a prophet, he would know who is touching him and what kind of woman she is — that she is a sinner."

Jesus answered him, "Simon, I have something to tell you."

"Tell me, teacher," he said.

"Two men owed money to a certain moneylender. One owed him five hundred denarii, and the other fifty. Neither of them had the money to pay him back, so he canceled the debts of both. Now which of them will love him more?"

Simon replied, "I suppose the one who had the bigger debt canceled."

"You have judged correctly," Jesus said.

Then he turned toward the woman and said to Simon, "Do you see this woman? I came into your house. You did not give me any water for my feet, but she wet my feet with her tears and wiped them with her hair. You did not give me a kiss, but this woman, from the time I entered, has not stopped kissing my feet. You did not put oil on my head, but she has poured perfume on my feet. Therefore, I tell you, her many sins have been forgiven — for she loved much. But he who has been forgiven little loves little."

Then Jesus said to her, "Your sins are forgiven."

The other guests began to say among themselves, "Who is this who even forgives sins?"

Jesus said to the woman, "Your faith has saved you; go in peace."

DISCUSS!

1. Of the main players in this story, what do you know about Simon?

2. What kinds of facts can you gather about the woman?

3. If Simon knew about the custom of greeting visitors with a kiss, and washing their feet, why might he have not practiced these upon Jesus' arrival?

4. What do you think motivated the woman to come to the dinner and crash the party?

___ For fun?
___ Insulting Simon?
___ Honoring Jesus?
___ Getting something out of it?
___ Something else?

5. This woman is called a "sinful woman"—in other words, she's a woman with a reputation. Today we'd call her a prostitute. Jesus knew well the Jewish purity law that said he'd become unclean because he touched a sinful woman. So why do you think he let a "sinful woman" touch him?

6. What was the main point of Jesus' story?

7. Imagine the feelings of Simon and the woman as the party began, and then as the party ended. Why would each feel this way?

8. Tell about a person who saw beauty, value, or potential in you before you saw it in yourself. How did it affect your life?

9. What does Jesus' unsolicited forgiveness say about him—and about the people who come to him?

REALITY CHECK

With whom do you identify most—Simon or the woman—and why?

Imagine that you are in this "sinful woman's" position. If Jesus himself saw through your profession or reputation to your beauty and then extended forgiveness to you, how would you be affected?

THE BLUE-COLLAR MAN AND THE IRS AGENT

ICEBREAKER

Gather together the want ad section of a local newspaper or two. Together as a group, scour them for the worst jobs—the ones you'd least like to have.

Tell about a time you changed jobs and ended up doing something very different than your last job. What were the greatest perks— and the greatest challenges?

You aren't the only one who has changed jobs. Just take a look at some of the people Jesus encountered in these stories. Because of him, their vocations weren't the only things that changed. Their hearts did as well.

Read Luke 5:1–11, 27–32

One day as Jesus was standing by the Lake of Gennesaret, with the people crowding around him and listening to the word of God, he saw at the water's edge two boats, left there by the fishermen, who were washing their nets. He got into one of the boats, the one belonging to Simon, and asked him to put out a little from shore. Then he sat down and taught the people from the boat.

When he had finished speaking, he said to Simon, "Put out into deep water, and let down the nets for a catch."

Simon answered, "Master, we've worked hard all night and haven't caught anything. But because you say so, I will let down the nets."

When they had done so, they caught such a large number of fish that their nets began to break. So they signaled their partners in the other boat to come and help them, and they came and filled both boats so full that they began to sink.

When Simon Peter saw this, he fell at Jesus' knees and said, "Go away from me, Lord; I am a sinful man!" For he and all his companions were astonished at the catch of fish they had taken, and so were James and John, the sons of Zebedee, Simon's partners.

Then Jesus said to Simon, "Don't be afraid; from now on you will catch men." So they pulled their boats up on shore, left everything and followed him.

After this, Jesus went out and saw a tax collector by the name of Levi sitting at his tax booth. "Follow me," Jesus said to him, and Levi got up, left everything and followed him.

Then Levi held a great banquet for Jesus at his house, and a large crowd of tax collectors and others were eating with them. But the Pharisees and the teachers of the law who belonged to their sect complained to his disciples, "Why do you eat and drink with tax collectors and 'sinners'?"

Jesus answered them, "It is not the healthy who need a doctor, but the sick. I have not come to call the righteous, but sinners to repentance."

DISCUSS!

1. What occupations did these people hold? List them, ranking them in order from most prestigious to least prestigious.

2. While in the boat, Jesus instructs Simon (Peter) to try for a catch one last time. Describe Peter's response to letting down the nets. What range of emotions do you think Peter felt at this time?

3. When the nets come up full, Peter reacts strongly. What does he realize about Jesus—and about himself?

4. What did Jesus mean by "catch men," and how do you think this vocational shift might appeal to fishermen?

5. Simon Peter, James, and John left everything to follow Jesus. What things would they have had to leave behind for their vocational change?

6. Before you discuss the second vignette about Levi, here's some information you should know: Of all people, tax collectors were the most despised by their countrymen. Why? Because the nation of Israel was occupied by the Roman army, and each family had to pay taxes to Caesar, the Roman ruler. So Romans hired Israelites to collect taxes from their countrymen and gave them the right to charge whatever they liked (which meant the tax collectors could keep whatever they made above the Roman tax). Therefore, tax collectors were really extortionist traitors. No wonder they were hated by all who came in contact with them.

Given this historical information, put yourself in Levi's (also known as "Matthew") shoes. How might you feel as Jesus—this popular rabbi, teacher, miracle worker invited you to follow him?

7. Do a cost-benefit analysis for Levi in his decision to follow Jesus. In what ways would he be better off—or not—in following Jesus?

Costs	Benefits

8. After Matthew chooses to follow Jesus, he decides to throw a party with all of his tax collector buddies and their unsavory friends. What would you say if you saw a priest or pastor hanging out at this kind of a party?

9. What does Jesus' response to the Pharisees say about his mission?

REALITY CHECK

With whom do you most identify—the Pharisees or the partygoers—and why?

Do your own cost-benefit analysis of following Jesus. How does it weigh out?

Costs	Benefits

Is there anything keeping you from responding to Jesus' challenge of "Follow me"?

PUTTING THE
PUZZLE TOGETHER

It was Christmastime at my in-laws'. As soon as I entered their home, I saw evidence that they were about to engage in one of their favorite pastimes—one thousand red-and-white pieces of a jigsaw puzzle strewn randomly across the dining room table. Upon closer examination of the individual pieces, I could tell how a few fit together, and that some sets belonged together. The edge and corner pieces were identifiable, but beyond that, the pieces were a jumbled mess!

That all changed when we grabbed the box top and displayed it prominently on the table. On the box was a photo of dozens of Coca-Cola collectibles that represented what the puzzle would look like once all the pieces were put together. By looking at the box top, we were able to get a much clearer picture of what our target was. We could look at each piece and see where it fit in the larger puzzle. With that box top, we were able to make sense out of the mess far more quickly!

Looking at snapshots of Jesus can be like staring at the mess of an unmade puzzle—very confusing. But looking at the box-top view of Jesus' life, teachings, and purpose helps to make sense of the smaller puzzle pieces included in this discussion guide. It will also give you a context for where those pieces fit into the whole puzzle, which adds richness and meaning to every individual piece.

So are you ready to plunge in?

One time Jesus challenged some prospective followers with these questions: "And how do you benefit if you gain the whole world but lose your own soul in the process? Is anything worth more than your soul?"[2] He wasn't content to let people live the ordinary cycles of life and work without carefully examining their purpose for living and the end results of their life.

Jesus' teaching was an amazing force that caused people to think and act differently. His insights were so wise and provocative that people changed the course of their lives when he spoke. He was highly sought out by people of every rank for his wisdom. But when he taught, Jesus didn't merely claim to be a good teacher or moral example. He claimed to be God-in-the-flesh. He claimed to personally forgive all sins, to be infinite over time, to be the one who had been prophesied about for centuries. He accepted worship and taught with the authority of God himself.

Jesus never desired to become a king or political leader. Instead, he served the people around him. He gave sight to the blind, strength to the infirm, and hope to the hopeless. His goal was not power, but servanthood.

His most important reason for coming to this planet was not to teach, to heal, or to be an example. He said his purpose was "to seek and to save what was lost."[3] He had come to establish a radical new community of formerly "lost" people who would love each other, share their resources, and build their lives on the principles of God. He called this group of people the "kingdom of God," and he invites everyone to join.

Jesus also realized, though, that this world—and every individual in it—had a problem. The problem was sin, our tendency to live our lives independently of God. Sin is our decision to follow our own judgments and morals, regardless of whether they agree with God's standards. It's putting ourselves, rather than God, in life's center position. Sin keeps us from enjoying life at its best and clouds our ability to relate to God.

But there's good news: Jesus came to reverse the curse of human sin. As a matter of fact, he told people over and over "your sins are forgiven."[4]

---

[2]Mark 8:36–37 NLT
[3]Luke 19:10
[4]Mark 2:5

CONCLUSION

The people whom Jesus forgave didn't know how this would happen. Nor did they know how much it might cost him. But Jesus did; he foreshadowed that cost when he said he had come "to give his life as a ransom for many."[5] Ultimately, Jesus knew that people's sins could only be forgiven if they were paid for by another source. And in doing so, God's cosmic laws of justice would be satisfied. People would gain the benefit of forgiveness and new life.

So who became that payment for the sins of the world? Jesus!

His life's purpose was accomplished at the end of his life. In spite of the fact he had never done anything wrong, he died a criminal's death, hanging on a Roman cross. This unjust death wasn't something he avoided or tried to escape from; it was the very purpose for which he came to earth. He wanted to trade his life for yours and mine!

But it gets even better. When Jesus died, he didn't stay dead. Just as he predicted five times, he rose from the dead the Sunday after his crucifixion, demonstrating his ultimate power over both death and sin. (We now call this "Easter Sunday.") He showed the world that he had the keys to life and death. And he validated his claim, "I am the resurrection and the life. Whoever believes in me will live even though he dies."[6]

In addition, Jesus left a challenge to all who might explore his life. He described the world as a place where people are on one of two roads.[7] Most are on a broad road of self-centeredness that ultimately leads to the destruction of the individual and those around him. However, a few make it to the narrow path that leads to life (both on earth and for eternity). But the only way to get on this path is through the gate of Jesus himself.[8] He promised that the benefits—joining the kingdom; having hope, joy, peace, and purpose; spending eternity with God—will come to those who rise to the challenge of choosing the narrow path.

When Jesus talked about an appropriate response to this challenge, he said, "For God did not send his Son into the world to

---

[5]Matthew 20:28
[6]John 11:25
[7]Matthew 7:13–14
[8]John 10:7–9

CONCLUSION

condemn the world, but to save the world through him. Whoever believes in him is not condemned, but whoever does not believe stands condemned already because he has not believed in the name of God's one and only Son."[9] To believe in Jesus is to rest the entirety of the weight of your life on him. It is to let him be the center of your existence and "bet the farm" on his claims to be God and to die for your sins.

If you are interested in being on the narrow path of life, Jesus invites you to join him. Tell him you are ready to join him. Admit you have lived a life centered on self, rather than on God. Tell him you believe that his death is your ticket to forgiveness. Ask him to help you rearrange your life so that he will be the central focus.

If you do these things, you'll begin the adventure of a lifetime—living hand-in-hand with the loving God of the universe! It will be a life with new love, new hope, and an eternal future— way beyond your wildest dreams!

[9]John 3:17–18

LEADER'S GUIDE

INTRODUCTION

These discussion guides are unique. Whereas most Bible discussion guides are designed for devoted Christians, these are designed for people in all different places in their spiritual journeys. Some may be committed followers of Jesus. Others may feel far from God. You may have a group member or two who are committed to another faith. Some may have been raised in a churchgoing family, but drifted away later in life.

Having a mix of people with a variety of opinions will make your discussions much more lively. Newcomers to Jesus will benefit from the experience of veterans, while old-timers will begin to see Jesus with fresh eyes.

The focus of all the discussions will be the life and teachings of the most influential person in the history of the world—Jesus of Nazareth. You'll be observing him through the biographical sketches of eyewitnesses—people who were there, friends who knew him. This series assumes that participants have little or no knowledge of these biographies, or of the rest of the Bible. The Icebreakers, Read portions, Discuss! questions, and Reality Check applications are designed to be accessible, fun, and provocative for all people—regardless of their spiritual journey.

The overall guidelines for the discussion are simple:

- The format is discussion—no lectures or sermons allowed.
- The leader will not primarily be a teacher, but a question asker and participant.
- Everyone is encouraged to participate. It's assumed that all have something to offer . . . and something to learn!
- Everyone's opinion will be respected, but feel free to politely disagree—it makes for better conversation and learning.

- No prior knowledge or religious experience is required. A diversity of experiences will be valuable to the group.

Most of all, have fun!

HOW TO LEAD A GREAT DISCUSSION

Want to have a terrific group, with quality discussions? There are two simple principles: learn how to ask and use questions, and make sure you're prepared ahead of time.

The Power of Questions

The biggest key to quality discussion leadership is asking great questions. The questions in this guide will give you a good start to a fantastic discussion. But you'll have to go beyond these questions if you want to have the best kind of group. Here are some principles for excellence in question-asking.

Use the Icebreakers. These questions will be ones that people from all kinds of spiritual backgrounds will be able to answer. They are critical to warm up the atmosphere, develop affinity between members, and create a sense of "group." They are lighthearted and geared toward getting to know people. They also serve to set up the discussion topic of the day.

Ask open-ended questions. Questions that only have a yes, no, or one "right" answer are a dead end for discussion. Even questions that are observation driven should begin with phrases like "Describe, list, recount, imagine, compare, or picture . . ."

Don't settle for a single answer. Most of the questions in the guides are multifaceted and will elicit many responses. For the questions that invite a personal response—especially the Reality Check questions—encourage many (or all) of the people to answer. Ask the same questions in multiple ways if need be. If only one person answers, try this response: "That's helpful. What does somebody else think?"

Probe for answers that go beyond the surface. Ask people, "Where did you first hear that idea?" or "Have you always thought that, or have your ideas changed over the years?" or "Where did you see that in the passage?" You may want to reflect back people's responses by summarizing, "So what I hear you saying is . . ." Another way to go deeper is to simply say, "Tell me more about that." You'll be amazed at the depth of responses when you listen well and ask follow-up questions.

Finish with the Reality Check questions. These questions are designed to make the content personal, bringing factual discussion home and helping the group to identify with the passage personally. Some of the studies have multiple Reality Check questions. You may want to select one, try all of the questions, or wing it, depending on how the group responds to your first question.

Feel free to deviate from the guides. Sometimes a particular question will need to be rephrased to fit the people in your group. So change the question! A question may get answered in the course of discussion before you even ask it. Skip the question! Remember, your goal is to create a discussion around the person of Jesus. Use the questions to facilitate that goal, but don't feel bound by the questions. Be a good conversationalist. Build on what people are saying and use questions to keep them focused on the main point of the discussion. Sometimes God may lead you to set the guide and your preparation aside, and follow an important issue the discussion raised.

Preparing for the Study

Normally leaders would spend about two hours in preparation and prayer for this kind of discussion. About five to seven days before the group meets, go through the study and familiarize yourself with the Scripture verses. Focus particularly on the key topic of the study. Allow yourself to see Jesus with fresh eyes. Imagine how group members might react to him. Let the truth of the passage sink into your own life.

Spend the next week watching for personal connections—illustrations from your life, news stories that relate, magazine articles, or movie clips. Integrate these illustrations at appropriate moments in the study. Nuance the questions or even change the Icebreaker questions to fit what's currently going on in your life, the nation, our culture (be sure, though, that it stimulates fun conversation and relates to the topic at hand).

Then, the night before the group meets, spend another hour studying the Scripture passages and preparing questions. Imagine yourself in the flow of the conversation. Figure out how to help the group understand the key theme. Craft your questions to bring out the best possible group interaction, understanding of Jesus, and focus on that key theme.

Then relax—and enjoy the group!

Note: The numbered questions in Discuss! correspond directly to the numbered questions earlier in the guide. However, not all questions will have a corresponding Leader's Note—only the questions that may have more difficult answers or need more direction. For more information on leading great discussions, check out www.zondervan.com/realitycheckcentral.org.

DISCUSSION ONE

THE PROFESSOR

KEY THEME

God sent Jesus to save us. The mechanism for this to occur is belief in Jesus. At that point we are "born again"—given a new spiritual life.

ICEBREAKER

The final scene of *Father of the Bride, Part 2* is both hysterically funny and deeply touching. The entire hospital scene is too long to show in this context, but there's a great six-minute clip that will set the great tone for the discussion. Begin where George and the doctor (Megan) are in the hallway. She says, "Mr. Banes, I'm concerned your wife is going to need to be delivered in the next few minutes."

End after he is holding his baby and the doctor says, "My pleasure." People may naturally comment on this great scene, but you need not go deep here. The following questions make for a great transition to today's discussion. If you don't have access to a TV, DVD, or VCR, just begin with the next question.

People love to tell baby stories, so take your time. After all, this discussion topic is about a birth—becoming born again. As group members share, look for parallel ideas and illustrations to bring into the discussion later.

Read John 3:1–21 • DISCUSS!

Question 1. Your group should be able to gather these facts from verses 1–2. Nicodemus was:

- A Pharisee—A sect of Jewish people who took following the intricacies of the law very seriously. They were distinct from Sadducees because of their belief in the resurrection.
- Of the ruling council—A member of the Jewish governing body with both spiritual and political power. Nicodemus was also respected as a "religion professor."
- Came at night—Perhaps he was afraid for his reputation.
- Teachable and curious—A terrific combination!

Question 2. After Nicodemus made his first statement, Jesus saw through to the real needs and questions of Nicodemus and began to talk about them. Nicodemus was an obvious spiritual seeker of truth and was even willing to take a risk with this radical new teacher from the north. Jesus' stimulating comment sets the tone for the rest of the conversation.

Questions 3–4. In discussing what it means to be born again, the most important point is to demonstrate that Nicodemus was thinking of physical birth while Jesus was talking about spiritual birth. Nicodemus' birth was from a mother, while Jesus' birth was of God. In our culture, people often consider those who call themselves "born again" to be narrow, close-minded, intolerant bigots. Or they may think the term refers to some touchy-feely religious experience that is largely indefinable. Whatever people bring up, be very careful not to judge—and be quick to laugh at yourself and at Christians in general.

If someone asks about verses 14 and 15, you can find the Old Testament account of Moses and the bronze snake in Numbers 21:4–9. Be sure you are familiar with this story as well, since it has parallels to Jesus and his purpose on earth. However, because of the limitations on time, don't delve into this subject unless a group member asks.

In the Numbers passage, the people of Israel are dying of snakebites. God commands Moses to fashion a snake of bronze and put it on a tall pole. He also says that when the people see it, they will not die of the snakebites. Similar to the snake, Jesus will be "lifted up" on the cross. All who look to him will find healing from the disease of sin and will no longer die eternally.

Question 6. Stick with John 3:16–18 for a while. In these verses, Jesus explains the heart of his identity, purpose, and message. Be sure group members see that God sends Jesus out of love, so that they may gain life. Notice the action words "loved," "sent," "not. . .condemn," and "save." Jesus is not about bringing about condemnation and guilt; he wants to reverse condemnation and guilt through saving the world. However, Jesus' new life takes effect only in those who believe in him.

Question 7. Assuming Jesus is God's Son, it is not arrogant, narrow, or intolerant to say he is God's only way. It is simply true. Point out that Jesus welcomes everyone—regardless of race, gender, education, or economics. All they must do is take God's provision for their inclusion in his family.

Question 8. In verses 19–21, light represents truth, embodied in Jesus. Darkness is the flip side of light—representing fear, evil, and deception. This might be a good time for some group comments on why people love dark ways. It may raise some habits, patterns, or reasons that some people in the group are not Christians. Probe for examples of how people have experienced this in real life. As you explore the breakthroughs that people have, be sure to be an encourager. Hopefully some significant breakthroughs will happen before this discussion is over!

REALITY CHECK

Turn the corner at this point to help group members do a little self-evaluation. When people compare their own search for God with Nicodemus', be sure to withhold judgment and ask questions that probe further into their own experience and spiritual journey. The idea here is just to get a temperature of where people are coming from, not to pressure them to change.

Watch carefully for how close people may be to Jesus and his truth. As you listen to their answers, you may want to follow up with certain group members privately, outside of group time.

DISCUSSION TWO

THE ROOF SMASHERS

KEY THEME

Our greatest need is the same as Jesus' greatest desire: the forgiveness of sins. Also, Jesus claims and demonstrates his deity.

During this discussion topic, the key is to help group members see their need for forgiveness and Jesus' power to grant that forgiveness. In addition to the great story of the paralytic, members will have the opportunity to view the sinful state of the world through a fun activity and their own fallenness through examining a "sin list."

ICEBREAKER

Bring a stack of *Time* or *Newsweek* magazines to the group. Ask people to find (or cut out) examples of how the world is messed up. Watch for the effects of sin (direct and indirect) and bring the list of those effects back when you get to the sin portion of the discussion.

If for some reason you cannot find or utilize the magazines, break the ice with these two questions:

- What is the longest line you have ever stood in?
- Was it worth it—and why?

If you decide to use the "longest line" question, try to draw out the sense of anticipation and excitement experienced in the line. Also look for the annoyances of being in crowds. Both of these factors will be relevant to the scene where Jesus does the healing.

Read Mark 2:1–12 • DISCUSS!

Question 1. The previous chapter, Mark 1, tells us about Jesus' reputation (in case anyone asks for that to be verified).

Questions 2–3. Allow people to utilize their imaginations. The details of the crowd, the motivated friends, and the surprise roof removal will provide a vivid backdrop for the unfolding dialogue.

Question 4. As you move toward the conversation between Jesus and the crowd, highlight the disturbing nature of Jesus' claim to forgive sins—especially in a monotheistic (one God) Jewish culture. These men had committed their lives to the belief in a single creator God, who had been worshiped by their ancestors for two thousand years. Only he could forgive sins. Jesus was now claiming to be this God . . . in the flesh. If people get hung up on the concept of the Trinity here, try this analogy: Steam, ice, and water are all H_2O, but in different forms. This simple statement can clarify the concept that Father, Son, and Holy Spirit are all God. Although analogies of the Trinity always fall short of the full nature of God, they can be helpful explanations.

Sin list–Question 5. Take a time out from the story in Mark to look at the "sin list." It's a great nonconfrontational way to help group members see their own moral deficiencies. Hopefully, everyone will agree that humans need to be forgiven. You need not discuss "original sin" or "total depravity" at this point. It's sufficient for people to admit that humans have a universal sin problem—and a universal need for forgiveness.

Question 6. It's striking that Jesus thinks the paralytic needs forgiveness more than healing. How much more is forgiveness the biggest need for able-bodied people! You may want to discuss how interpersonal forgiveness releases hatred and heals relationships. Forgiveness from God clears up the haze that has clouded our potential for a relationship with him.

Questions 7–9. After this, move back to the passage. Allow the physical and emotional tension of the moment to become clear as Jesus claims deity with the irritated and critical Jewish leaders looking on. Help the group experience the climax of the healing—and feel the emotions and minds of the audience shifting as they became eyewitnesses to the change in the paralytic.

REALITY CHECK

The first question encourages group members to consider their own—and others'—perfection. And when they do so, they can't help but realize how imperfect they are, compared to Jesus.

As people think about the "sin list" and how they stacked up against it, they will be convinced of their own sin without you hammering the issue. In addition, they'll have to wrestle with the question of Jesus' deity. Like the audience who was with Jesus, they will probably have mixed emotions and opinions. Although you shouldn't force conclusions, let members leave a little disturbed by Jesus' claims and actions. Such thoughts and emotions will encourage them to think about God's standards—and their own failings—over the next week. And it will set the stage for craving the relief and joy of receiving Jesus' forgiving power.

THE CORPSE

KEY THEME

Jesus demonstrates power over death. This validates his claim that whoever believes in him will live, even though he dies. His compassion also gives us a window into his heart for people.

Two very important themes run through this passage.

The first is that Jesus holds power over life and death. He predicts Lazarus' resurrection and then pulls it off. Wow! If there is anything to validate his claims to be God, this is it!

Second, Jesus acts with amazing compassion, weeping even though he knows he is about to do a miracle. This story can really help people in pain understand how Jesus reacts to them during their darkest moments.

ICEBREAKER

Although this Icebreaker can be a bit heavy, it brings great insight on a person's view of God during his or her most vulnerable moments. Watch carefully for ways that group members might connect with the hearts of characters in this story—especially Mary and Martha.

Read John 11:1–45 • DISCUSS!

Question 1. Using only this story, we can learn a great deal about Jesus' relationship with Mary and Martha. Take time here to show how much Jesus loved Mary, Martha, and their brother Lazarus (verses 3 and 5). Uncover Martha's great faith in Jesus' miraculous powers (verses 21 and 22). Point out that Jesus wept with them in the midst of their pain (verse 35). All of these statements point to the conclusion that this relationship was not a casual acquaintance, but a deep, loving friendship. And yet Jesus waited two days to go and see the sick Lazarus. Why? Plant this "why" question in group members' minds, then continue with the next question.

Question 2. Obviously, from verses 8 and 16, we know that Jesus and the disciples risk their lives when they return to Judea. Clearly the disciples aren't excited about going back. Thomas, in particular, throws out a scathing bit of sarcasm in response to the idea.

Yet Jesus doesn't seem disturbed. Why? Here is some insight into verse 9: "The connection of thought here is that the hours of the day are not affected by external circumstances. They are there to be used. The implication is that Jesus' hour has not come (i.e. the 12th hour) and until God wills that it should come, the only course to adopt is to go about one's mission."[10]

Question 4. In verses 25 and 26, Jesus is referring both to the resurrection of Lazarus and the resurrection of all people at Judgment Day. Jesus often makes supernatural claims about the spiritual world just before his supernatural acts in the physical world. In this case, the resurrection of Lazarus validates his claims to be able to one day bring life after death to all who trust him.

Question 5. If your group has trouble with why Jesus cried at the tomb, but not when he received the news of his death, point them to verses 4, 15, 23, and 42. Jesus clearly was not sad about Lazarus' death because he knew he would raise his friend from the dead. However, he was especially moved (verse 33) by the pain that gripped the people around him. This moment in the study can be particularly poignant for people who wonder, *Where is God when life hurts?* The answer is that even though Jesus knows the end of the story, he weeps right along with people who are in pain. Why? Because he loves each one of us intensely. This point may be the most important—and stunning—to some of your group members, so don't be afraid to dwell on it.

Question 6. As your group encounters the resurrection scene, let their imaginations roll. Don't stick to strict rules of observation

------

[10]Taken from *The New Bible Commentary: Revised John*, by Donald Guthrie (Grand Rapids: Eerdmans, 1970), 953.

here, but allow your group to fully experience what it must have been like to watch Lazarus come out of the tomb.

Question 7. This final multiple choice can be very useful in helping group members wrestle with the heavy implications of this historical matter. It will also give you a good barometer reading on their stage of openness or skepticism.

REALITY CHECK

Begin this section by bringing the compassion of Jesus into the group members' current realities. Gently refer back to the Icebreaker time and invite people to contemplate what Jesus' reaction was to their situation (paralleling their experience to Mary and Martha). Understanding that Jesus weeps with us in the midst of our real pain can make all the difference when life is dark.

The second question is a process question, not a truth question. Listen carefully as group members describe where they are in their spiritual journey. Be careful to withhold judgment, yet, at the same time, watch for cues that can make for good one-on-one conversation in another context.

DISCUSSION FOUR

SOLDIERS AND CRIMINALS

KEY THEME

Jesus' behavior as he died on the cross points both toward the credibility of his claims to be God and the meaning of his death (to reconcile people to God).

ICEBREAKER

Be sure to handle this opening question with sensitivity and grace. Our culture doesn't always talk about death openly, but seeing someone in their dying days reveals volumes about their true character. Listen with a sympathetic ear and be ready to make reference to these stories later as you discuss how Jesus handled his own death.

Read Luke 23:32-49 • DISCUSS!

Questions 1-3. Jesus' composure and other-centeredness during his crucifixion is a compelling reason to believe that he really is God. In times of pain and in the face of death, most people react harshly to others. They are looking only for comfort. But those watching Jesus saw a very different attitude. Examine Jesus' response to the guards, the other people at the crucifixion (verses 35-39), and the two criminals.

These first three questions should reveal how unusual Jesus' response to his own torture and death is.

Question 4. The first criminal assumed that Jesus was not in fact God, as he claimed to be. The other presumed that he was God. Their reactions—and eternal destinies—were diametrically opposed as a result.

Questions 5-6. It's critical to emphasize here that the criminal did absolutely nothing to earn a place in heaven. As a matter of fact, I think we'll all be surprised by the kind of riffraff who make it into heaven. The key here is not the morality of the criminal's life, but his response to Jesus. He recognizes who Jesus is and responds in faith to what he knows.

A person can never be moral enough to get into heaven. Never. No matter how much good we do on this earth, we are always a mixture of good and evil—a kind of Dr. Jekyll and Mr. Hyde. The critical question for us is not, "Have we done enough good things?" but, "Where will we find mercy and forgiveness for the ways we have hurt others and betrayed God?" The second thief saw that the answer was right in front of him—at the cross of Jesus. Jesus died on the cross to pay our death sentence for our sins. Amazing! He died so we can be forgiven.

Our relationship with God cannot be bought or earned. We can only get right with God by trusting Jesus' death to pay off our extensive debt of sin.

Everyone is a moral criminal. We are all guilty. But the world can be divided into two categories—those who recognize Jesus and trust him, and those who mock him or walk away.

Question 8. Not only should Jesus' credibility be apparent through his death, but you'll also have the opportunity to highlight how his death brings reconciliation between people and God (while discussing the curtain tearing).

Here is some additional information: For 1500 years, since the time of Moses, the people of Israel were dependent on the high priest to make atonement for the people. This happened through animal sacrifice and through asking God for forgiveness. Once a year the high priest would enter the "Holy of Holies." He could only approach the presence of God with great fear. It was here that he could ask for forgiveness on his own behalf and on behalf of all the people. When the veil was torn, access to God was no longer reserved only for the high priest. It became available to everyone. Using the diagram of the temple will help you address this important point.

Question 9. The centurion is only one of the people who responded to Jesus' death, and he was stunned by what he saw. He had probably seen hundreds of men crucified, and recognized the excellence in the character of Jesus in a time of intense duress. During this study, be sure to highlight the different responses of the people to Jesus' death. Each gives a valuable perspective. Group members will probably identify more strongly with one character than another.

REALITY CHECK

The "personal reaction" question will give you a glimpse into each individual group member's heart and mind. It's a fabulous opportunity to see where people are coming from. Some might be skeptical, while others may be very open. At this point, some might be interested in an invitation to trust Jesus' death on their behalf. If so, it's a great time to ask them to read "Putting the Puzzle Together" on their own—or with you. Then make an appointment to discuss it with them one-on-one.

Also, you'll want to help people imagine what an everyday experience with the living God might be like. Jesus claims to have made this possible through his death (thus the curtain tear). This kind of accessibility to the Almighty is unique to the world's religions. It's the greatest part of being a follower of Jesus. A present, loving Father-God brings a warmth and intimacy to the cosmos. It also provides a degree of company, comfort, and purpose in living that carries with it a joy that goes beyond words. Help group members "try on" this idea—to see just how attractive faith in Jesus is.

DISCUSSION FIVE

THE PROSTITUTE

KEY THEME

Nobody is beyond the reach of God.

ICEBREAKER

A casual discussion about blowing money and extravagant gifts should set the stage for this story of a woman who possibly spent all she had (one biographer says "a year's wages") on a bottle of perfume.

Read Luke 7:36–50 • DISCUSS!

Questions 1–4. The brilliance of this story is in the clear contrast between Simon and the sinful woman. On the one hand, take Simon, the Pharisee. He's a man who has given his life to following the law, trying to be moral, and obeying God's commands. And yet he cannot see God when Jesus is right in front of his nose!

The woman, on the other hand, is known for her sinful lifestyle. Yet when she sees Jesus, she knows he is special and embodies hope for people like her. The beauty of Jesus is that he identifies with the woman (not with Simon) and clarifies the situation with a riveting illustration.

Use the first four questions to draw out the stark differences between these two compelling characters. Explain to your group that the Pharisees are a religious sect that believes righteousness is earned by meticulous observance of God's laws (revealed through Moses, but greatly expanded by Jewish teachers). Simon was also certainly among the most upstanding citizens of his community.

Question 5. After comparing Simon and the woman, turn your attention to Jesus. As usual, Jesus sees through the artificial social constructs (in this case, moral reputation) to the heart of the person. He immediately understands the woman's actions in the context of gratitude.

The story is made even more powerful by this historical background: If Jesus did touch a woman like this, he would be considered by Jewish law to be ritually unclean. He'd need to go through ritual washings and purity rites before he was allowed to go into the temple or experience other facets of life. Religious people of Jesus' day scrupulously avoided becoming unclean—not only because of the inconvenience, but also because of the social stigma.

Question 6. Jesus tells this story to explain the sensibility of the woman's actions. Her tears, perfume, and devotion are understandable because of the magnitude of forgiveness. Jesus isn't saying that Simon doesn't need forgiveness, and Simon's lack of hospitality shows it's obvious he probably hasn't experienced Jesus' forgiveness. Possibly, he isn't even aware of his need.

Question 7. After discussing the story, it's time to get a bit more personal. Here, Simon would have his whole concept of righteousness shifted. From his background as a Pharisee, he always would have assumed that righteousness was earned through religion and morality. Then he finds out that righteousness comes through forgiveness instead. It might be good at this juncture to point out that no matter how righteous we are, we still need forgiveness for our wrongdoing.

The woman, in contrast, must have walked away with a fresh sense of her new lease on life. She was probably jubilant—transformed not only for her life, but also for eternity.

Question 8. As people become cognizant of the way the sinful woman felt after the dinner party, allow them to discuss how having people believe in them has caused their personal transformation. Although the sharing of stories may take a while, the time spent will be well worth it and full of touching moments.

REALITY CHECK

For the first question in this section, there may be different applications for people in your group—depending on the person they identify with. By this point, it should be fairly easy for them to come up with an application just by associating themselves with a character in the story.

If there is time, ask those in your group to put themselves in the woman's shoes, to imagine the experience of forgiveness from their own perspective. Some group members may never have imagined the feeling of true forgiveness. Imagining may be a very powerful and important tool for their spiritual journey.

DISCUSSION SIX

THE BLUE-COLLAR MAN AND THE IRS AGENT

KEY THEME

Count the cost when you decide whether or not to follow Jesus.

ICEBREAKER

Your group will have fun looking through the want ads for the worst kinds of jobs. Because people normally look for jobs they want, this will be fresh and can be a lot of fun. If you cannot get your hands on some want ads, simply brainstorm a list of the occupations in our culture that, justified or not, get a bad rap. What jobs do people least want to do, and why?

Whichever option you choose, it will be great fun to discuss jobs nobody likes! The laughter alone will warm up the atmosphere. In addition, you'll later be able to relate some of these comments to the common, redundant fishing occupation or the despised occupation of tax collecting that you'll discuss later in your group time.

Having group members share about the jobs they've had also gives you insight into who they are, as well as their likes and dislikes. And it sets the stage for them identifying with "The Blue-Collar Man and the IRS Agent."

Read Luke 5:1–11, 27–32 • DISCUSS!

Question 1. Jobs in the passage, best to worst, are:

- Teacher of the law
- Carpenter (Jesus)
- Fisherman
- Tax collector

Teachers of the law were not always professional teachers; however, they were highly regarded in their community for their role in understanding and explaining God's law. Carpenters and fishermen would be the trades in the middle of the pack (although carpenters smelled better!), and tax collectors were the lowest-regarded humans in Israel because they served a foreign government and charged excessive rates to their countrymen.

Question 2. In verse 4, Simon Peter may be skeptical because:

- He had tried and failed.
- It was not the optimal time for fishing.
- What did this carpenter know about fishing?

However, the important point is that he obeys because of the teaching and miracles of Jesus.

Question 3. After the big catch, Peter realizes that Jesus is God. It's clear evidence to a fisherman that if Jesus can control the fish biting, he must be divine! He also realizes that he himself is morally bankrupt before this perfect God-man. Realizing his unworthiness, he says, "Get away from me!"

Question 4. By "catch men," Jesus was making reference to being in the "people industry" and catching others in God's nets.

Question 5. Imagine the challenges of this job transition! Instead of boats, nets, and early mornings, your tools are words, people, and group gatherings. You move from blue-collar work to ministry. It's a risk to become dependent on the gifts of others. Many people in your group will be able to sympathize with the difficulty of this shift in vocation.

Question 6. Matthew was probably overwhelmed with pride that he was singled out by this religious leader. He may have been delighted to leave the guilt of extortion behind him to find a fresh life in the miracles of this man. However, I'll also bet he felt a fair degree of ambivalence in leaving a lucrative job to follow a homeless preacher around the Middle East.

Question 7. In the cost-benefit analysis question, unearth some issues that could be *very* difficult for the three fishermen and the tax collector to give up in order to follow Jesus—financial security, the safety of their everyday existence, being with their families, the vocation they know and love, the communities they grew up in, control of their lives, or the admiration of friends. You can also encourage a lively discussion of the benefits of following Jesus. Draw out practical things like friendship, teaching, healing, and being close to Jesus, as well as intangibles such as adventure, hope, meaning, joy, love, and peace.

Questions 8–9. In this story, Jesus shows up at a party filled with the dregs of society. It's easy to imagine how critical the very conservative Pharisees would be of Jesus' action. However, it is here we learn a key lesson from Jesus: he is most interested in healing people who realize their ailment, not those who are aloof. Help people understand that the key difference was not that the Pharisees had no sin, while the tax collectors did. The difference is that the tax collectors knew of their spiritual need, while the Pharisees denied it.

REALITY CHECK

Moral people might identify more strongly with the Pharisees, while those who engage in wild living might identify with the tax collectors. The key here is to help all group members realize their need for forgiveness.

At this point, you can really challenge the group to follow Jesus. First, help them count the cost of following Jesus. Their costs may include time, money, approval of family and friends, particular sins or dreams they'd have to give up, and most important, control of their lives.

At the same time, you can point out the benefits. Simon Peter, Andrew (the assumed partner in the other boat), James, John, and Matthew loved their new life with Jesus so much that they never turned back. They were so full of joy that years later they would rather go to their death than give up following Jesus. It could be the same for the people in the group!

So make sure you take time—as a group or individually—to address any of the remaining barriers group members have to following Jesus.

CONCLUSION

PUTTING THE PUZZLE TOGETHER

At certain junctures in the life of your group, you'll want to use a tool to clarify the central message of Jesus' teaching and the central reason for his visit to our planet. The "Putting the Puzzle Together" section will help you at these junctures. It's a tool designed to be versatile enough to be used in a variety of circumstances:

- If people are demonstrating openness to experiencing the sudden impact of Jesus, you may want to point your group members to read it on their own.

- If they ask what the main message of Christianity is, it may be better to sit down and discuss it together (you can read it out loud together or silently—whatever feels most comfortable—and then discuss it).
- It might serve as a great answer to a question that comes up during group time or one-on-one conversation after the group meeting.

Read "Putting the Puzzle Together" carefully and use it strategically as relational opportunities arise to discuss how Jesus' life and death intersect the lives of your group members. If they are interested in getting on the narrow path, let them know that their first step is to talk to God about it. Offer to pray with them. It may become a conversation that changes their life . . . and eternity!

ACKNOWLEDGMENTS

I am bursting with gratitude to all who made these guides possible. So many people have contributed to this project that it would be impossible to thank them all. However, some who have made an exceptionally large contribution rightfully deserve to be acknowledged.

Thanks to Garry Poole and Mark Mittelberg for opening the doors for these guides to be published. Tim Anstead was a great asset in web research. Hundreds of leaders field tested the material in earlier forms and gave great feedback. InterVarsity at the University of Illinois pioneered new ideas, tools, and strategies. Willow Creek has provided an entirely new platform for the Reality Check series to be utilized. My dream editor, Ramona Tucker, took these guides to an entirely new level with passion and professionalism. Most of all, I'd like to thank Kelle Ashton for bearing the weight of extra home duties, putting up with scores of late nights, and believing in me—long before anyone else did.

Thank you all!

Willow Creek Association
Vision, Training, Resources for Prevailing Churches

This resource was created to serve you and to help you in building a local church that prevails!

Since 1992, the Willow Creek Association (WCA) has been linking like-minded, action-oriented churches with each other and with strategic vision, training, and resources. Now a worldwide network of over 6,400 churches from more than ninety denominations, the WCA works to equip Member Churches and others with the tools needed to build prevailing churches. Our desire is to inspire, equip, and encourage Christian leaders to build biblically functioning churches that reach increasing numbers of unchurched people, not just with innovations from Willow Creek Community Church in South Barrington, Illinois, but from any church in the world that has experienced God-given breakthroughs.

WILLOW CREEK CONFERENCES

Each year, thousands of local church leaders, staff and volunteers—from WCA Member Churches and others—attend one of our conferences or training events. Conferences offered on the Willow Creek campus in South Barrington, Illinois, include:

Prevailing Church Conference: Foundational training for staff and volunteers working to build a prevailing local church.

Prevailing Church Workshops: More than fifty strategic, day-long workshops covering seven topic areas that represent key characteristics of a prevailing church; offered twice each year.

Promiseland Conference: Children's ministries; infant through fifth grade.

Student Ministries Conference: Junior and senior high ministries.

Willow Creek Arts Conference: Vision and training for Christian artists using their gifts in the ministries of local churches.

Leadership Summit: Envisioning and equipping Christians with leadership gifts and responsibilities; broadcast live via satellite to eighteen cities across North America.

Contagious Evangelism Conference: Encouragement and training for churches and church leaders who want to be strategic in reaching lost people for Christ.

Small Groups Conference: Exploring how developing a church *of* small groups can play a vital role in developing authentic Christian community that leads to spiritual transformation.

To find out more about WCA conferences, visit our website at www.willowcreek.com.

PREVAILING CHURCH REGIONAL WORKSHOPS

Each year the WCA team leads several, two-day training events in select cities across the United States. Some twenty day-long workshops are offered in topic areas including leadership, next-generation ministries, small groups, arts and worship, evangelism, spiritual gifts, financial stewardship, and spiritual formation. These events make quality training more accessible and affordable to larger groups of staff and volunteers.

To find out more about Prevailing Church Regional Workshops, visit our website at www.willowcreek.com.

WILLOW CREEK RESOURCES™

Churches can look to Willow Creek Resources™ for a trusted channel of ministry tools in areas of leadership, evangelism, spiritual gifts, small groups, drama, contemporary music, financial stewardship, spiritual transformation, and more. For ordering information, call (800) 570-9812 or visit our website at www.willowcreek.com.

WCA MEMBERSHIP

Membership in the Willow Creek Association as well as attendance at WCA Conferences is for churches, ministries, and leaders who hold to a historic, orthodox understanding of biblical Christianity. The annual church membership fee of $249 provides substantial discounts for your entire team on all conferences and Willow Creek Resources, networking opportunities with other outreach-oriented churches, a bimonthly newsletter, a subscription to the *Defining Moments* monthly audio journal for leaders, and more.

To find out more about WCA membership, visit our website at www.willowcreek.com.

WILLOWNET (WWW.WILLOWCREEK.COM)

This Internet resource service provides access to hundreds of Willow Creek messages, drama scripts, songs, videos, and multimedia ideas. The system allows you to sort through these elements and download them for a fee.

Our website also provides detailed information on the Willow Creek Association, Willow Creek Community Church, WCA membership, conferences, training events, resources, and more.

WILLOWCHARTS.COM (WWW.WILLOWCHARTS.COM)

Designed for local church worship leaders and musicians, WillowCharts.com provides online access to hundreds of music charts and chart components, including choir, orchestral, and horn sections, as well as rehearsal tracks and video streaming of Willow Creek Community Church performances.

THE NET (HTTP://STUDENTMINISTRY.WILLOWCREEK.COM)

The NET is an online training and resource center designed by and for student ministry leaders. It provides an inside look at the structure, vision, and mission of prevailing student ministries from around the world. The NET gives leaders access to complete programming elements, including message outlines, dramas, small group questions, and more. An indispensable resource and networking tool for prevailing student ministry leaders!

CONTACT THE WILLOW CREEK ASSOCIATION

If you have comments or questions, or would like to find out more about WCA events or resources, please contact us:

Willow Creek Association
P.O. Box 3188, Barrington, IL 60011-3188
Phone: (800) 570-9812 or (847) 765-0070
Fax (888) 922-0035 or (847) 765-5046
Web: www.willowcreek.com

REALITY CHECK SERIES
by Mark Ashton

Winning at Life
Learn the secrets Jesus taught his disciples about winning at life through the stories he told.
Saddle Stitch
ISBN: 0-310-24525-7

Jesus' Greatest Moments
Uncover the facts and meaning of the provocative events of the final week of Jesus' life.
Saddle Stitch
ISBN: 0-310-24528-1

Leadership Jesus Style
Learn the leadership principles taught and lived by Jesus.
Saddle Stitch
ISBN: 0-310-24526-5

Hot Issues
Find out how Jesus addressed the challenges of racism, feminism, sexuality, materialism, poverty, and intolerance.
Saddle Stitch
ISBN: 0-310-24523-0

When Tragedy Strikes
Discover Jesus' perspective on the problem of suffering and evil in the world.
Saddle Stitch
ISBN: 0-310-24524-9

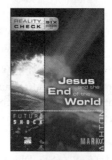

Future Shock
Uncover Jesus' perspective on the mysteries of the future as revealed in the Bible.
Saddle Stitch
ISBN: 0-310-24527-3

Sudden Impact
Discover the life-changing power of Jesus as he interacted with his contemporaries.
Saddle Stitch
ISBN: 0-310-24522-2

Clear Evidence
Weigh the arguments for and against the Jesus of the Bible.
Saddle Stitch
ISBN: 0-310-24746-2

www.zondervan.com/realitycheckcentral.org

GRAND RAPIDS, MICHIGAN 49530 USA
WWW.ZONDERVAN.COM

www.willowcreek.com

Tackle the Tough Questions

Tough Questions Series

By Garry Poole and Judson Poling

Foreword by Lee Strobel

Tough questions. Reasonable questions. The kinds of questions that require informed and satisfying answers to challenges against the Christian faith.

Each guide within the **Tough Questions Series** spends six sessions dealing frankly with a specific question that seekers and believers often ask about Christianity. These thought-provoking discussions will help your group find answers and discover how reasonable the Christian faith really is.

Question 1: How Does Anyone Know God Exists?   ISBN: 0-310-22225-7
Question 2: Is Jesus the Only Way?   ISBN: 0-310-22231-1
Question 3: How Reliable Is the Bible?   ISBN: 0-310-22226-5
Question 4: How Could God Allow Suffering and Evil? ISBN: 0-310-22227-3
Question 5: Don't All Religions Lead to God?   ISBN: 0-310-22229-X
Question 6: Do Science and the Bible Conflict?   ISBN: 0-310-22232-X
Question 7: Why Become a Christian?   ISBN: 0-310-22228-1
Tough Questions Leader's Guide   ISBN: 0-310-22224-9

*Look for the **Tough Questions Series** at your local Christian bookstore.*

GRAND RAPIDS, MICHIGAN 49530 USA

WWW.ZONDERVAN.COM

RESOURCES

www.willowcreek.com

The Case for Faith

Lee Strobel

Was God telling the truth when he said, "You will seek me and find me when you seek me with all your heart"?

In his best-seller *The Case for Christ,* the legally trained investigative reporter Lee Strobel examined the claims of Christ, reaching the hard-won yet satisfying verdict that Jesus is God's unique Son.

But despite the compelling historical evidence that Strobel presented, many grapple with doubts or serious concerns about faith in God. As in a court of law, they want to shout, "Objection!" They say, "If God is love, then what about all of the suffering that festers in our world?" Or, "If Jesus is the door to heaven, then what about the millions who have never heard of him?"

In *The Case for Faith,* Strobel turns his tenacious investigative skills to the most persistent emotional objections to belief, the eight "heart" barriers to faith. *The Case for Faith* is for those who may be feeling attracted to Jesus but who are faced with formidable intellectual barriers standing squarely in their path. For Christians, it will deepen their convictions and give them fresh confidence in discussing Christianity with even their most skeptical friends.

Hardcover	ISBN: 0-310-22015-7
Softcover	ISBN: 0-310-23469-7
Evangelism Pack	ISBN: 0-310-23508-1
Mass Market 6-pack	ISBN: 0-310-23509-X
Abridged Audio Pages® cassette	ISBN: 0-310-23475-1
Unabridged Audio Pages® cassette	ISBN: 0-310-24825-6
Unabridged Audio Pages® CD	ISBN: 0-310-24787-X
Student Edition	ISBN: 0-310-24188-X
Student Edition 6-pack (with Leader's Guide)	ISBN: 0-310-24922-8

Pick up a copy today at your favorite bookstore!

ZONDERVAN™

GRAND RAPIDS, MICHIGAN 49530 USA

WWW.ZONDERVAN.COM

WILLOW CREEK RESOURCES

www.willowcreek.com

Mark Ashton is the director of seeker small groups at Willow Creek Community Church. In addition, Mark supervises the staff for more than forty new believers groups and Willow's Internationals ministry. He is also the director of *TruthQuest*—Willow's ministry that answers tough questions about Jesus and Christianity. Mark is a frequent speaker at conferences and is the author of *Absolute Truth?*

For more information, go to
www.zondervan.com/realitycheckcentral.org.

We want to hear from you. Please send your comments about this book to us in care of the address below. Thank you.

GRAND RAPIDS, MICHIGAN 49530 USA

WWW.ZONDERVAN.COM